HOW T
WITH KIDS
ATTITUDES

Ultimate Strategies to Control Difficult Children and Make Them Listen

By

Ann R. Sutton

COPYRIGHT

ZeroNever Publishing House

USA | UK | Canada

Table of Contents

CHAPTER 1 - INTRODUCTION

Raising children is like grooming a dwarf tree; it needs so much attention and so, to be successful as parents, we have to look after our precious little ones consistently to be sure they do not become our most dreaded nightmare.

Children are amazing, but what about the ones with attitude? Now, every child will show off some bad character at some point in their lives. If they do not show it when they are four, you will see it when age eight arrives, and if you escape them at 8, they will catch up with you at 12 (oh! The most dreaded one!). When they do, will you still find them to be amazing?

How do you manage your kid's attitude? Do you get exhausted because they are busy growing up? If you do, then this will help you. I hope you find answers to the questions in your mind.

CHAPTER 2 - SIGNS YOU ARE RAISING A KID WITH A BAD ATTITUDE

As parents, there is no way for us to escape raising children with bad attitude. This is because every child between 0 and 18 years has a trace of bad character; it will inevitably show up though it may be more conspicuous at a certain age than the others. With this, we should buckle up to get them back to the right track they started.

There is a difference between a child that shows off a bad attitude and the one that has a bad character. The difference is that the one that shows off a bad mood may just be having a terrible day. Maybe his team lost in soccer because he missed the goal he was supposed to score, or it could be that her favorite toy fell off the counter and broke. This behavior is not so for a child with a bad attitude. A child with a bad attitude will always exhibit these negative behaviors despite the day, time, or situation.

The following signs will help you know if you are raising a kid with a bad attitude:

1.   Consistent negativity

Negativity is prevalent in kids, but you need to know when your child is just a child, and when he is flipping over to the back page of life. Stirring rudely and feeling terrible about the plate of veggies before him is normal but when he is negative even after you've just showered him with many beautiful gifts, know there is something wrong, and you have to investigate what it is.

Kids usually become cynical if they are in a negative home or if their dominant temperament has negativity as a conspicuous trait. Also, your kids reflect the state of your marriage, and if it is not so good and you and your spouse continually have these crazy fights, your kids will not be happy.

2.   Your child acts and speaks disrespectfully to people in authority

This is a trait to expect in almost every child especially when they are in their teenage years, and those who suffer directly from this are those with authority over the child such as the parents, teachers, and the rest. Children start to display this attitude by talking back or answering rudely. The more introverted type may do it the passive way by just ignoring the person or murmuring. This behavior can so drive a person nut.

3.   Your child always does not do as you say

This character is outright disobedience and rebellion. Kids that do this will also speak rudely to you. I know your kid can forget what you instructed, but if the child keeps repeating it and you know for sure that they are not suffering from amnesia, then that kid has a bad attitude.

4. Your child consistently whines and complains about everything

It is very saddening to see the child you love so much and do everything to make a comfortable pout, whine and complain. You have to learn not to give in to every pouting, whining, or crying even it comes with rolling on the floor and kicking things. Do not give in.

When children whine and complain, they want their parent to give in and do things the way they want. You will notice that your teenager is always complaining about a family weekend or get together and approach it like that is the last place they would like to be. It is common, almost every parent has experienced this and those who gave in never obtained a good result.

5. Your child fights about everything

This is not addressing the little disagreements; it is resolving the conflict between you and your child in your home. If you notice this behavior in your child, know that your child is in a real power struggle with you.

Do not be tempted to argue with him; you will end up not addressing the real issue. Giving in will make the child happy; they already know how much it takes to wear us out. Ignoring the child will also do you no good. He may get inside and bang the door, and it feels like everything is okay until another day when he is more prepared; you will be wondering if he took his time to plan for you.

6. Your child does not dare to face life

There are times we all fall on our faces due to one disappointment or the other. Children also have this time. However, as humans, we should gather some courage and bounce back. If your child gets down for not making it to the football team, the cheerleader's group, or any form of disappointment; and does not make any effort to get back on his feet, know that there is an underlying attitude problem. Failure should give them the courage to try harder and not continually sulk through life.

7. He/she is too carefree about life

This is a big deal, and as a parent, you must find out why your child is not just taking anything seriously in life. Kids usually become carefree when they have encountered failure or the disheartening experience that comes with disappointment. Most kids take up the carefree attitude as a way to make them feel safe.

This character could also be caused by sending too much criticism to your child's way with little or no encouragement thereby making them feel they do not need to try so hard to do anything right since there is a huge possibility that you will not praise them for it.

8. He/she does not take responsibility for the things he does wrongly

"...but I didn't cause this!" "It wasn't my fault". Every parent has heard these phrases, and though there are times they are correct, there are also times they are not. We all believe our children can never hurt a fly and cannot do anything wrong; the truth is, they do. Remember when your parents could swear that you could never be disrespectful when you knew deep down that you have done that more than once? It's the same thing.

9. He/she is selfish and does not care about any other person

A child can be selfish every once in a while; this is normal. It is also okay if your child that is two does not know the importance of having an arm stretched out to give. However, if you notice your child in elementary school or even grade school barely shares what she has with anyone, you need to do something.

Being selfish does not only end at sharing things; it can affect the other areas of their lives and even develop a deep sense of jealousy and envy. This attitude can make your child fell terrible when her friend spends time with another, or if she sees one of her siblings with a thing that belongs to her. Continuing this way will make her feel like she is the only one that should receive all the love and care you have to offer.

10. He/she always has a feeling of entitlement

The world today has led children to believe that they are entitled to everything you have given them and even the ones you do not have to offer. It looks like it is reasonable and also the parents believe the same. However, this is not true.

How do you know you have an entitled kid? This kid is one that will cry and have an outburst of emotions when you do not give him what he wants nor do things their way. He will confidently break all the rules because he believes they are for everyone but him. With this kind of character, your child will never be grateful for the things you do and will always demand you do more till there's nothing more, you can do.

11. He/she is always playing the victim

Having a child that still plays the victim can be irritating, and some of the times, you will even have to believe they indeed are. You will frequently hear your child say "that's too difficult for me to do", "I just can't play with him, he's mean to me", etc. This is so not a funny thing to handle.

CHAPTER 3 - WHY YOU NEED TO DEAL WITH KID'S LOUSY ATTITUDE

A child without discipline is like a city without walls. As good as children can be, leaving them to drown in their horrible manners can be compared to you pouring some gas around your house and waiting for the right time to light fire. A disaster! That is what it could be.

There are many reasons we should discipline our children; some of them are:

1.   Discipline is a great way to show them, love,

We keep our favorite clothes safe and well preserved from dirt and moth; if anything comes on it, we ensure we take it out till the last spot. It is same with children. Discipline takes out the dirt that could make them less precious to us as parents and to the world at large. Giving your child the right dose of training is like creating a world of their own and handing them the keys.

In other words, discipline is like a mold in which our children are poured in and allowed to set; it helps shape them for a better life.

2.   It helps them stay safe

When kids learn what is right for them and work hard to keep doing those things, they will always be safe. Imagine a kid that lost an opportunity to play with his toy because he cunningly assessed the knife and played carelessly with it. If his parents explain that the blade is sharp enough to hurt or even kill him and lay consequences for this life-threatening act, he will find a way to caution himself.

Keeping our kids safe with discipline does not involve us scaring them with lies; the idea is to help our children set positive milestones that will help them get through life. Just painting the right picture of an alligator is to keep your child far from them as much as they can forever.

3. It helps them develop self-control

When a kid gets the right dose of discipline, he can have total control over himself. When a child learns how to manage anger and frustration the right way from his parents, he can never battle with anger issues again. He will also know how to look away from things they cannot get since they know life is not all about them.

A disciplined child will grow to become a person with integrity since they won't be affected by everything they see. If it is with food, they know how to lock up their throats and if it is with money, they will know how and when to spend it.

4. It helps them know how to treat others appropriately

When a child is disciplined, he will learn (through the right teachings of his parent) the importance of treating others well. For instance, if the child had to face the consequences for talking back rudely to a teacher in school, that child will know that talking back to older people or people in authority is not so good and to avoid the consequences, they will do all they can to stop.

Getting a good dose of consequences mingled with the right proportion of teaching and correction will help you groom a child that is respectful and considerate.

CHAPTER 4 - WAYS TO DISCIPLINE YOUR CHILD

Whether your child quietly ignores your instructions or boldly looks into your eyes with his legs stamped to say "no" to the very thing you've said, they are all disrespects, and as much as we have discussed, you should know that you cannot let it slip before s little flame turns into the big fire that pulls down your roof.

It is our duty as parents to discipline our children, but this task can be so overwhelming, especially because some children do not just want to give in. It can be so upsetting that we may want to beat the living hell out of them.

Now, must we always spank children? Is that the best way to make them learn? We will answer that as we proceed but for now, let's see how to discipline our kids.

The following tips will help make parenting a less tedious task for you as a parent.

a)   Treat it as soon as it comes

Like we discussed earlier, do not blink at a wrong attitude and do not procrastinate handling it. Shifting it to another time will make you unable to treat it like you should because the effect has worn down. It does not matter if your kid is just two or has grown to twelve, let them know you do not accept their wrongdoings, and you will not bend the rules for them. Doing this will help them understand what to do and what to avoid so that when they grow up; they won't be fearless enough to try it.

b) Keep your cool

Children can so step on your toes till you start considering the best way to show them how much they have ignited your anger. However, it is essential to let them know they do not have so much power over you. Your kid after studying you for w while will be able to pinpoint the things that make you shout and most of the times, and He will deliberately annoy you to get that shout.

My neighbor's eight years old son deliberately leaves the dining table after eating. He does this continually because he knows that his mum will get pissed and nag till the entire neighborhood knows something has gone wrong. Imagine this; never let your kids push you to that level. If they are so keen on getting the worst from you, surprise them by keeping your cool while devising a perfect punishment. Trust me; they will never have the courage to mess with you again.

c)   Let them see the respect you desire

Children learn faster by copying what their parents do. Do you and your spouse disrespect each other? Know that your kids are watching and very soon, they will start disrespecting you two. Avoid fighting in the presence of the kids; you know every issue can be settled in the bedroom. Do not forget that your children's brains are magnetic, and they never let an unfortunate word slip. Will you be surprised if you hear your four years old say to her friend "never you screw with me again"? Are those words common to you or your spouse?

Also, do not be tempted to be your child's assistant. Show him you expect him to do his homework and keep his room clean and avoid being that reminder for him. If he forgets, the consequences will remind him the next time.

d)   Let them know your expectations

Don't quietly scrub the toilets hoping your kid will know he has to help you clean the windows since its Saturday morning. Let her know what your expectations are as a parent. Be clear in your approach but not forceful.

Children in their pre-teenage and teenage years do not like being pushed around, but as a parent, you know you must be able to get your way. If you need the windows cleaned, don't say "are you too daft to know that today is Saturday and the windows deserve to be cleaned?" Instead, try something like "I need your help to clean the windows. Can you do that for me?" and you will watch them happily make your windows squeaky clean.

e) Attach consequences to offences

The consequences that help the child grow more are the ones that have direct connection to the crime. For example, if you child refuses to clean his room when you ask him to, let him know that you will have him clean it when he is supposed to be out playing soccer with his friends. If he refuses to do his homework, let the alarm wake him up 30 minutes before time to do it.

As long as your child knows he has to give up something he loves as a result of his offence, he will have no other option than to be more compliant.

f) Never accept an excuse

Excuses will groom your kids to become procrastinators in life. If your child keeps forgetting to return the library books till they are past the time, do not listen to "I forgot" or "I was too busy to have realized it was past the time"; let the fee come from their monthly allowance.

Accepting excuses will only make them find more ways to keep skipping duty. We just can't let that. A child must learn to do what he must do even if it means them getting up at midnight to do it.

g)   Carefully consider every decision you make

Remember how you felt when your youngest walked out on you without even giving a second thought to what you were saying? How did you feel? I'm sure you felt like locking up the room and throwing the key into the deepest river. Now, what do you think would have happened if you did that? You would have been the one to pay the carpenter to change the locks and bring your sweet adorable daughter out.

The same thing happens when we make permanent decisions in the heat of anger. Kids will always step on your toes, and you must avoid taking their offence to heart. Keep your cool and do the right thing. The time will pass.

h)   Refuse to be a part of that debate

The only thing arguing with those little things that came through you can do for you is to shift the attention from their offence to your anger. In the end, you will lose. They will always come for a debate to piss you off, but you have to show them they can't get you.

i)   Choose your fight

Even the strongest warrior gets exhausted if he fights every battle that comes his way. It does not mean you should allow the child to be free from the consequences; it means you should know when your child's attitude should get you talking, and when it should not. If your three years old does not want to stop hitting her toy on the floor, do not bother; as long as she knows, she will not get another once that one breaks.

j)   Let them earn

Children will always be mindful about the money they worked to acquire. You should sometimes pay them for doing a little extra from their regular chores. If you are not comfortable with this, give them their allowance. It's okay to provide them with a bit of stipend to take them through the month. When they know they won't get more when the one at hand is exhausted, they will learn how to save.

k)   Keep improving on the rules

As your child grows, there will be a need for more freedom and trust. Feel free to give them the little space they require. Trusting them will help them build their self-confidence. If you did well with their training when they were younger, they should be good to go.

It does not mean you should give up on the rules, no! Find a better way to enact them; they too must be tired of the same old method.

CHAPTER 5 - DISCIPLINE STRATEGIES FOR SPECIFIC BAD BEHAVIORS

a) If he is disrespectful to people in authority

When kids show this attribute, you need to punish the kid as a parent. Also, you have to check yourself to see if you talk disrespectfully about another person in authority like your parents, even your husband.

This situation should be handled by making the child have a better view of authority. It is okay to punish, but it is essential to talk to them about the implications of their deeds.

b) If he ignores your instructions

Do not unleash your anger on the child and do not keep begging the child to cooperate with you. If you do, you won't get the desired result. The surest thing that works here is defining boundaries because your child needs to know that he or she is in your home and you and the other parent are the only people in charge, so there is no need for the power struggle.

c) If he always whines and complains about everything

Do not be tempted to cave, stand your ground and as long as you are their parents; he will follow anywhere you desire. Whether with a frown or a smiley face, you will still achieve your goal, and he will learn to adjust.

If it is about a family get together and he doesn't want to come, assure him that it will be fun and that he will enjoy him then turn back and head to the car. He will follow.

d)   If he fights about everything

This issue is best handled by setting clear boundaries and attaching suitable punishments for any breach. Whenever he commits, be prompt to enforce the positive behavior and punish the offence. Do not be complacent about this. The more consistent you are; the better tour chances of turning him back to the frequency you desire.

e)   If he does not dare to face life

To help your child through this kind of situation, allow him grieve whatever caused their disappointment for a few days and after that, walk up to him and be a source of encouragement. Try not to preach about how the frustration happened; do not even say how disappointed you are yourself; that is not what he needs to hear. Asking him the way forward will help him realize that there is a way out.

If there is another opportunity to try, teach him what he needs to do to make it this time. If there is none, encourage him to try out something else with a more positive attitude. Your child will have a better view of life and failure once you teach him never to give up.

f)   If he is too carefree about life

Sometimes, a carefree attitude could be a symptom of low self-esteem. Children with low self-esteem believe he does not have what it takes to make it, so he gives up trying. And since failure caused them pain, he uses the carefree attitude as a shield to prevent them from future strains.

This kind of child will likely not do anything until someone pushes him. That is your job as a parent. Give him a little head-on, and he will start moving in the right direction; we all do need that every once in a while.

g)   If he does not take responsibility for his wrong deeds

Before hitting hard on your child for this behavior, be sure you are not encouraging it in a way you do not know. Do you find yourself blaming the teachers, coaches and even his friends without really listening to their side of the story? Then you are helping the child shift blame.

Make your child learn to accept his mistakes; without this, there will be no way for him to the corrections and change his attitude.

h)   If he is selfish

If your kids just don't let anyone have a share in what he has; teach them the need to share. Also, always request he share their foods and toys with their other siblings and friends. It will help them learn.

i)   If he has a feeling of entitlement

You must teach your children that everything you do for them is out of love and not because he is entitled to it. It will help root out the ingratitude in your child, and he will learn to value everything he receives from you; even the little lollipop.

j)   If he is always playing the victim

You have to ensure you do not run in every time your child claims a thing is "too difficult". Let him find a way to do the things that are seemingly difficult so that he will know he is an overcomer. Let your child know how to achieve something by himself. When he starts crossing little barriers, he will build as much courage as that needed to slay a dragon.

ADVERSE EFFECTS OF HARSH WORDS AND SPANKING ON A CHILD

If raising a good child is your aim which I believe it is, you have to shift your focus from punishing their bad behavior to teaching them how to do well. It does not mean you should not punish bad behavior; it means your parenting should not just concentrate on that.

Do you spank and use harsh words on your child? What about yelling? If you have, then it is essential, you know that these things can influence a child negatively instead of correcting them. Let us take a look at what spanking, yelling and speaking harsh words do to a child:

- **Spanking encourages aggressiveness in children**

Spanking has made children more aggressive instead of correcting them. According to a study performed on children 20 whose families reside in large cities in the united states, the children who were frequently punished and spanked by their parents grew up to misbehave the more thereby causing their parents to beat them the more.

From this research, spanking did not correct the behavior; it gave them the courage to do more (because they gradually grow used to the spanking and eventually believe they have seen the worst, so there is no need to change).

Spanking affects the parent-child relationship and breeds hatred in a child's heart for their parents instead of love. Spanking a child is causing him/her pains and children who get beaten most likely transfer the hurt to others by speaking hurtful words or hitting them. Do you see why some kids fight when they do not get their way?

- **Increased level of toxic stress**

Physical punishments put a child at risk of injuries which can leave marks on the body of a child. The results of these punishments are worse for children who are barely older than 18 months. Spanking children also increase the level of their hormones which are related to toxic stress. Spanking can hinder the development of their brains. There is a study that showed a young adult who developed a lesser grey matter (the brain part which influences self-control) and also has a lower IQ test result because of repeated spanking. Comparing this result to other young adults who were trained with other means aside spanking, theirs were better,

- **Harsh words abuse!**

Like spanking, harsh words cause pains. The only difference is that spanking causes physical hurt while harsh words cause emotional harm, which usually require too much effort to be healed. Abusive words can also cause shame in children. Children who faced abuse find it difficult to meet up with their peers in the competitions of life. This is because harsh words cause them to develop low self-esteem, which automatically stunts their growth.

Doctors say spanking a child increases the child's risk to develop a mental disease and in as much as we are trying to correct our children, we should ensure we do not leave everlasting scars in their lives.

CHAPTER 6 - HOW TO MAKE THEM LISTEN

Kids are busy! They are always busy trying to get it right with their video games and Barbie's hair. Getting their attention when they are in this state can be so fruitless if you do not know how to go about it. Want to get your kids to take in what you say, do it this way:

1.   Catch their attention first

Since these little aunties and uncles we gave birth to are too busy trying to figure out what their toys will have for dinner and how they can be the most out to their football, you must ensure they notice and pay attention to you before you say a word; else, it will be a fruitless effort. So how do you achieve this?

The first thing is for you to move close to your child, take notice of what they are doing. You can say "that braid looks good on Barbie", you know she'll look up to say thank you. There you can get her. Take that opportunity to connect by making eye contact. Right here, feel free to say what you have to say.

As a parent, you are familiar with your child, and you know just how to draw their attention. Do not forget; you can get them to notice and assimilate what you are saying without you having to shout. The louder you shout, the lesser they hear.

2.   Say it and be quick about it

Do not forget these little creatures have a lot on their mind and like when talking to a person in business, say what you have and do it quick. If you don't, they will switch back to doing what they were, and you will have to battle with getting their attention again.

This means you should carefully screen your statement to ensure you have taken out all the unnecessary words and phrases. I'd you wanted to say "don't you know you should stop playing by now or do you think the homework will do itself" gently say "oh darling, you should put that down and get to your homework". That will spare you the stress and get your words into their heads at once.

3. Resist the temptation to nag; I meant to say, 'repeat yourself.'

If your child didn't get you the first time and you want to sink it his skull, refuse to repeat yourself. Doing that will make you lose his attention more and will eventually turn you into the nag you have so tried not to be.

If your sweet cutie does not hear you, it means you either didn't get their attention or you lost it. Either way, you have back to step one.

4. Give them your attention else you will lose theirs

Their focus can be very short-lived and to make the most out of it; you have to give them yours too. If they realize you are looking sternly into their eyes, they will have to take their minds from what they are doing and sow it back to you. But if you fail to give them your attention, you won't even notice when they have given you theirs, and in any way, you lose.

5. Don't order, don't beg! Find a balance

Try to understand their feelings; how do you feel when your boss walks in to give those stupid orders with his shoulders almost being higher than his shoulder pads? I guess you immediately fell like punching him in the face. I know the last thing you feel in such a situation is the motivation to act out his orders.

Kids also feel the same way. A child won't feel like punching you in the face, they will only feel like they have trespassed, and this will make them less willing to perform according to your orders. So how do you still put your words across when you do not beg or order?

6.   See it through their eyes

In their eyes, what they are doing is essential, and so they can't understand why you are so hung up on them arranging their room right now. I mean, the place is okay, and everything is well displayed for you to locate what you need without having to pull out any cupboard.

So to get them to do what you are doing, you have to address them according to the level of importance they have placed on their current activity. If your child was braiding Barbie's hair and you want her to clean the room, say "I know you are doing a great job with Barbie's hair but why don't you go clean up your room so Barbie will have a nice room to sleep in tonight?" Oh, dear! You just coaxed open her heart and she will dump Barbie and run over to ensure the room is well arranged for her sweet little plastic to sleep. Hmm!

7. They can corporate if you click the right button

The thing with getting kids to listen is doing what you have to for them to corporate with you; else, it will be very frustrating. To make the corporate, you have to find a way to make them see that what you want them to do it essential either for you, for themselves or anybody they love and if they see that the need to do it is higher than the thing they are currently doing, they will corporate.

It is not because for them, dismantling their puzzle is more important than taking the breakfast that will facilitate quality growth in them. For this reason, you have to be able to coin your words to get them to have a change of mind.

8.   Let the above tips have its effect on you

If you have closely followed the above tips, you will notice that all of them teach you to be

- Patient
- More calm and serene
- Very understanding.

These are critical factors in parenting, and if you possess these qualities, parenting will be a lot easier than you think.

CHAPTER 7 - ANGER MANAGEMENT TECHNIQUES FOR KIDS

Every human being could get angry, and every once in a while, they get mad. However, if a person let's anger overwhelm him to the point that it leads him to speak or act otherwise, then there is an anger issue.

Kids are human beings though a less mature version. They too get angry. Like every other human being, kids can develop anger issues. The following traits usually characterize these anger issues:

- Inability to control temper
- Throwing things around when biting
- Hitting, biting and inflicting pain on others when they do not get their way
- Becoming unable to make any explain himself due to the heat of the anger
- Blaming others for the harm they caused when angry.

There are other irregular ways kids express anger and to help your kid manage his passion correctly; you have to understand him and learn what works best for him.

The following are great strategies to help children calm down their anger. Try some of them on your child and watch out for the effects; eventually, you will get to pick the most suitable one.

1. **Teach them how to take a deep breath**

Adults who use this strategy to calm anger and anxiety can testify about the potency of deep breaths. Apart from calming irritation, it helps send down more oxygen to your body for better metabolism.

This strategy can also work for your children, but it will need some work from you as a parent. You have to know how to approach your child to teach him how to take the deep breaths. Teach him to take at least three deep breaths at a time after which he can rest and get to the next round. He should be able to gain control over himself before getting to the fifth round.

When he has mastered the art of deep breathing, remind him to do that every time he is angry and eventually, it will become a habit for him.

2. Help them build some anger vocabulary for better anger expression

Some kids tend to act violently as a way of expressing anger; however, this can be managed if you teach them a better idea of expressing themselves. Teach your kids how to use words like 'annoyed, angry, mad, irritated, anxious, nervous, agitated, etc.' to express their anger.

If they still find it difficult to express themselves after learning the words, give them a little push by reminding them what to say. Encourage them to say things like "I'm agitated because..." or I feel outraged because ..." and they will pick it up from there.

3.   Get them to a calm place

Encourage your child to go to places like the park or garden to relieve the anger. If there is no such place around or you do not feel okay with them going out alone, encourage them to imagine a calm and serene place.

If you have artworks that convey serenity, encourage them to look at it and try to find meaning from there. This strategy will work better if you are not the cause of their anger.

4. Let them write out what makes them feel so mad

Writing needs patience, and as a child takes the time to write out one word after the other, the anger will also be leaving one after the other. Depending on your child and is temperament, he may be able to gain control of himself before he finishes his writing.

When your child expresses his anger on paper, it will save you or others from being the direct recipients of the violence. If he wants to get aggressive, let him do it with the words on a paper through his pen and not through his mouth.

5.   Encourage him to tear out the written anger

If your child does not still gain control of himself after writing, encourage him to tear the paper carrying the written anger into pieces; he can do that with all his strength like he is fighting the cause of his wrath. This technique will work very much for an aggressive child.

6.   If they the sensitive kind, encourage them to draw or paint

The sensitive children prefer to cry and throw things around when angry, and this is because the anger affects the deepest parts of their hearts and causes them real pain. So to relieve their pain, they cry like they sustained a severe injury.

To help this kind of child, encourage him to draw or paint. This drawing will help him visualize his pain, and before he finishes, he will find a way to admire the colors on the paper; the anger will fade.

Many creative children tend to draw or paint very amazing works when they are angry or sad. Depending on your child's personality, his anger can be his muse. You never can tell.

7.   If they are the hyperactive kind, get them a punching bag

Have you ever gotten a call from your child's school reporting that he beat another child blue-black? If yes, get him to use this technique. Since he loves to punch, get him something he can hit till there is no more strength and since punching can cause him some pains on his hand without any physical effect on the punching bag, he will find a way to relieve his emotions and learn to stop hurting himself with anger.

This technique has worked for only some classes of kids, because there is a suspicion that this technique can cause some children to become more aggressive and impulsive as they grow. Observe your child and immediately get him to stop if this technique does not make him better.

When you find a suitable technique for your child, encourage the child to keep doing that every time he gets angry. Doing this will become a habit for him, and he will not have difficulty controlling his anger as he gets older.

CHAPTER 8 - DEVELOPING POSITIVE THINKING IN CHILDREN

Parents are usually the first to be directly affected by negativity in kids. It can be so sad to have your child grown dark daily instead of reflecting the love you have so showered of him and before we go on to find the solution to negativity in kids, let us look at the possible causes of this negativity.

Kids usually find negativity to be a more comfortable place for many reasons. Some of them are:

• You give too much criticism and very little appreciation and encouragement
• They do not find the peace and love they require to grow into better beings at home
• You or your partner is always negative
• They have some psychological issues
• You are overprotective of them.

Kids who do not have or believe they do not have the privilege to air their views will develop low self-esteem and will turn to negativity. This negativity will hinder the child's growth and take away the joy of childhood. Imagine growing up and having nothing spectacular about your childhood.

The good thing about this negativity on kids is that there are things you can do to help as a parent. To help your child, do the following:

1.   Get close to them

There is so much your closeness to your kids can do for them than you could imagine. Getting close to a child has been proven to solve discipline issues that shouting and punishment could not explain. When you get close to your child (not as a fierce parent but as a friend and one they can trust), you will hear their heart cry. You will even see what makes your child afraid.

It may not be you; maybe it is their consistent inability to what their mates are doing. Imagine a child that has been sent to summer school twice because he failed in school? He cannot be happy. He wants to be like others and be seen as a bright child with prospects too. Go close and listen.

2.   Let them know they have a say

Negativity can so reduce a child's self-esteem to nothing till they begin to think that being dead would do their parents better. You surprised to believe a child could feel that way? It's possible, I've thought of it a thousand and one times. Let them know you that you will love to hear what they think about any topic, and when they know that their opinion is valid, they will open up more to you.

Granting them self-expression can be the most significant thing you could do to help them out. With this, your child can be open to tell you what makes him cry at night. That rebellion is not for nothing.

3. Love could be all they desire

Kids are fragile, and no matter how stubborn they claim to be, they still need someone to hold them close. Do not be surprised if the very insolent child wants to be sure you love her.

This experience is a widespread one for busy parents. Parents who do not have time for their kids find out their kids develop resentment and stubbornness. In a case like this, love is the response. Do not fight, don't fret, give them your time and show them how much they mean to you, and they will find their way to becoming healthy again.

4.   Be their #1 fan

Everybody needs encouragements; that is why football players and participants in every game appreciate people coming out to watch and root for them. Your kids are not an exemption. Many things can make your kid demotivated, and when these things come their way, you are the closest person to remind them they can do it.

Learn when to scold your child and when to motivate the child. If that kid wanted to help you replace the plate on the counter but mistakenly broke it, do not scold; he already feels incapable of doing anything right. All he needs to hear is "sweetie, I know you wanted to help and what happened was just a mistake; don't worry, you will be able to help me as much as you want next time". What motivation. That child will know that you understand his intention and that you believe in him. Next time, he will be eager to help and will guard the plate with both hands so that nothing in this world happen to it.

5. Let them know that the law of attraction is real

The concept of the law of attraction helps us understand that our minds are magnetic and so our subconscious mind can bring to us whatever our thoughts dwell on.no kid truly wants to be a failure so when they ponder on the possibility of failing, tell them that their subconscious mind can bring to pass whatever they ponder on. A child that behaves like mine will swap.

6.   Keep them around positive people

Our friend has a high power to influence the way we think and do things. To help your child become positive, be sure he has positive people around. As a parent, I advise you have an eagle eye and do not hesitate to separate your baby from any negative child; you can't risk it.

Take your child to great sites like museums, parks, and the rest where they can see and meet happy people, and they will be encouraged to live a positive and happy life. No stress!

7.   Teach them to find the solution and not dwell on the problem

Your child will see this to be as an easy task if you, as the parent, focus on the answer to issues alone. If you are the kind that goes about sulking and lashing out on everyone because you have a problem, know your child will not listen to you on this.

Children learn by examples, and our kids are a reflection of who we are. If you are a positive person, your child will be the same, but if you are negative, you have to work on your negativity first.

When your child has a challenge, encourage the child to think about ways to solve it. It's okay if they cry at first about the problem, but when they finish, you should help them to pick up their pieces and find a way to get out of the mess. This singular act will train them to become ethical leaders in future.

8. Trust them with a little bit of freedom

Giving your child some freedom is a sign that you trust them. I know they have to spend an hour after their dinner reading an exciting story with you to improve the bond, but you have to spare them some time to build relationships with their friend too.

Bad things will not always happen. Let your kid ride the bicycle with his friends around the yard; there is no written law that a child must fall and break his legs every time he gets on the bike.

Also, learn to spare your children some crap. You have lived in this world longer than they have; I know but then let them learn to do things their way. If it works, out, they will know they can do something good, and you will learn from them, but if it fails, they will come back to doing it their way.

Being positive has a lot to do with how much a child believes in himself.

CHAPTER 9 - ACTIVITIES TO HELP YOUR CHILD DEVELOP POSITIVE THINKING

K ids can easily switch from negativity to positivity when they are involved in mind-blowing events. These events will help them lighten up without much effort from their side because all they will need to do is to enjoy the fun of positivity; yes, positivity is fun!

Since one of the best things we can do to help our children with negative thoughts is to teach them how to process their feelings from a positive light, the following activities will be helpful.

1. **Share positivity with them**

Doing this is the most important thing. Since our kids are tender, anything we say can hurt them, and most of the times, our kids turn out to be who we say they are. Have you noticed? Parents who use harsh words on their kids tend to raise terrible children.

Be kind to your children, forgive them and do not inflict pain on them. They will be great if you say they are. I know they can be annoying but believe me; we were same to our parents.

It has been discovered that kids from loving families have better self-image compared to those from broken or angry homes. Keep your home in good shape and be an example for your kids. With this, you will be amazed at the level of positivity they will acquire.

2.   Helping others

Helping people do not only do good to the person receiving the help; it is also beneficial to the person offering it too. Like adults, when children help people, they develop this sense of self-worth and love. Doing this can help your children have a better attitude and feeling towards himself.

Indeed, people who volunteer hardly fall into the trap of low self-esteem and they generally have a better outlook of life compared to those who do not. Letting your child help others will make them feel happy and very optimistic about life.

People who regularly help others say helping others make them feel inner peace and joy; they said they do not struggle to have a sense of belonging and to be grateful. When a young child helps, she puts herself in the shoe of the person in need of help, and this will help her develop more love for others.

Getting your children to help others is not that much of a difficult task; getting them to improve their neighbors or siblings pick toys would do. They can assist their grandma in the kitchen or even render help an older woman to do a little of her chores.

This little acts of kindness have a great ability to make our children positive, and the more they get involved in them, the more their level of positivity will increase.

3.   Let them meditate about loving-kindness

Meditations have been to transform the lives of many. It has helped many discover the path to purpose and peace in life. This meditation can also be helpful for your child that is battling with negativity. Meditating about loving-kindness won't help your kids become more positive in life, it will, of course, improve their health and mindfulness of being.

The loving-kindness meditation has to do with your kids setting their minds on their loved ones and sending some positive thoughts their way. As the child proceeds, she can start adding other people to the class of those to get positive thoughts from there.

For this meditation, let them focus their minds on one person at a time to send positive thoughts. The most frequent positive thoughts to be addressed are those of happiness, safety, and ease through life.

4.   Keeping track of amazing moments

Happiness is gotten from the excellent little moments of our daily lives. Your child can be lightened by remembering some fantastic moments in their lives. To help them do this, get them a little book and pen; if she likes, she can call it the "awe journal". This tip is not for children only; you too can keep one as a parent.

In this journal, you and your child can take notes of the beautiful sites you see and the sweet activities you get involved in daily. They do not have to be significant. If your child loved when her uncle made her sit on his neck, let her write it down. Whatever brings good feelings to a person is welcome to this journal; even the smell of your paternal grandma's freshly baked cookies.

This book is meant to be expressive. Feel free to describe the scenario and if making an actual drawing will help you retain the memory, please draw.

I know you may wonder how this act can help make a person feel positive. The thing is, writing down your positive experiences will help you and your kid to be more mindful of the positive things happening around you.

This book should always be close by so that you and your child can refer to it when you feel down and discouraged. You never can tell how much the smell of your child's paternal grandma's freshly baked cookies can boost your child's positivity.

5. Let them learn how to set and achieve new goals

I would have said let them learn how to dream and wish, but this alone cannot get a child the positivity she deserves. There is joy in doing, and there is fulfillment in accomplishing your goals. The enthusiasm obtained from wishing and dreaming is usually short-lived if not backed up with actions to make them a reality.

Encouraging your child to set goals and achieve them can be easy. She can start by picking one of the things she has always wanted to do for herself. This activity can be painting her favorite cartoon personality or just anything. Guide her on how to male plans for it (which will include getting the drawing and painting board as well as the paint and brushes to be used). Let her go-ahead to visualize the possible distractions that could hinder her success and keep them away. When she finishes, let her execute her plan.

The joy she will have will be equivalent to the one you do when you pull down something that was seemingly difficult in your workplace. It is life, and we all gain courage by doing things we never thought we could.

6.   Let them learn a new skill or language

Learning a new skill or language allows them to develop their abilities. Learning something new does not only improve their expertise; it helps take a child's mind away from the triggers of her negativity. Just like in school, learning a new skill or language will help a child do #4 and experience the joy of being successful.

Getting a child to learn this new skill and expand her horizon will also help a child build confidence in her. This much-needed confidence will help her face the world boldly and live her life without so much fear of the unknown. Having a confident child is like raising a superhuman. They know they can do it, and they do it in ways you could have never imagined.

7. Let them have some positive affirmations

Positive affirmations are those positive words a person can keep declaring to help them develop courage and good self-esteem. These words are healing, and they have helped many people from negativity to positivity.

Getting your child to come off with some positive affirmations of their own can help them become positive. Is there a time they feel they are not equal to the task? Let them affirm themselves. Teach your child to say things like 'I can do it", "I am more than enough", "I know I am adequate", etc. and they will see themselves slowly becoming that which they proclaim. If they have more, let them be free to add. The more the affirmations, the quicker their positivity level will rise.

CHAPTER 10 - TIPS FOR EASIER PARENTING

Parenting can be a very tedious task, especially if you do not have external help. Your children are blessings to you, but you have to find an easy way to make raising them a bit less stressful and fun to you.

The following tips will help you go around parenting the better way:

- **Get them involved in the chores**

Getting your child involved in chores, of course, can only work when your child attains age two. The children may not be able to do so much actual work, but getting them to concentrate on one thing will give you the freedom to do another. This deed will also help them develop the concept of help, and as they grow, you will always have a helping hand.

- **Create a healthy routine**

You can also call this routine habit. Your works will get more comfortable as a parent when you get your kids to know what they are supposed to do and the exact order they are supposed to do them. Let them know that when they wake up in the morning, they are supposed to dress their beds, brush their teeth, take their bath, comb their hair and carry their already arranged school bags downstairs. Establishing this routine will prevent you from nagging and shouting out every atom of energy you have.

You can create this routine by writing them down and attaching it to the walls of their rooms. When they wake up, encourage them to read it and act accordingly. When they master this unchanging schedule, your only work as a parent for that moment will be to ask them "have you brushed your teeth?' 'is there another thing I can do to help?' and the rest. You see, this is a real pathway to rest for parents.

- **Establish a sound discipline system**

Having a good discipline system can help keep you from nagging them with the rules daily. Let them know the consequences that await them when they go against the rules and stick to them. When they get used to this system, you will be living with them like you are living with some semi-adults (at least in that aspect).

- **Create a bond**

Parenting can never be fun without this aspect. Children bring joy and sometimes, the most significant help you need in parenting is to have a reason to do it with pleasure. Having a close bond with your child will help you know what to do for him at the right time.

With this, even when they do not lift a finger to help you in the house, you will find the task easy to accomplish alone. Remember when they were still infants, they didn't need to do anything to help you. Only seeing them smile was enough to give your energy the most desired boost to be superhuman; it can still be same now.

Delight in your kids and parenting will be the best job in the world.

CHAPTER 11 - HOW TO USE AUTO-SUGGESTION TECHNIQUES FOR IMPACTING KIDS

Auto-suggestion techniques have helped develop self-control and confidence in adults. It has helped many draws in their breaths and stays in control of their subconscious mind. Have you ever told yourself to calm down that all will be well? If you have, then auto-suggestion has been working for you for some time now. This article will teach you how to control your kids with the most powerful tool, which is your mind.

The law of attraction is real, and auto-suggestion teaches us how to use it for our favor Auto-suggestion can be a great way to have an impact on your child. Since it is not so easy to get and keep the attention of children, you should learn how to impact them even when you have just a minute to make your point.

Also, auto-suggestion is vital to determine the outcome of your children. This fact is actual because what we think and say about them tends to come to pass (remember the law of attraction), so you can use auto-suggestion to transform their lives

Applying this great tool will help you get their love and obedience; it will also help you build a better relationship with them. The following auto-suggestion techniques will help you:

1. Consciously take away negative thoughts

Negative emotions and feelings will always arise when we have a not so pleasant experience. As a parent, you may think wrongly when your child proves stubborn or disrespectful in some ways, but if you replace the negative thoughts with positive ones, you can stand a chance to change your child's attitude without much stress.

If your child keeps pushing your buttons, deliberately refuse to be annoyed with the child. Try to take out a moment of your day and think to yourself of how you would love the child to be and claim the possibility of it. You can request the potential of a better behaving child by thinking: "this child will be obedient", "he will get to love how to clean his room", "he is the best child ever', etc. The more you think positively about your child, the more they will transform.

Aside from this helping your child transform, it will also make you a more positive person.

When you have a positive outlook of life, your children will copy and become positive too. This act will ease your parental struggle in two ways.

2. Use positive affirmations

Positive affirmations are an excellent replacement for negative thoughts. Positive affirmations keep us calm while attracting what we are affirming. Have you ever heard that the tongue has the power of life or death? If you have, then you should be able to apply your language with wisdom. Speak what you want to see, not what is happening.

When your kids get out of the way, do not only complain about how they turned out; speak how you want them to be, and they will adhere to you. Say things like 'my child is smart', 'my child is healthy', 'he is the best child in the world', 'he is hardworking and intelligent', etc. Saying all these positive things about your children will help bring them to the state, you want them to be. Are they having difficulty academically? Use positive affirmations, and they will get better.

You should use these positive affirmations both in front of them and when you are alone. Saying it in front of them will give them the zeal to become better; it will also be an excellent neutralizer for the negative criticism you send their way. Meanwhile, affirming them when you are alone will help you build confidence in them. This confidence will empower your kids to be a better version of themselves and will also help you to do all you can to make them better.

Meditation can also be a great time to use a positive affirmation. While connecting to your innermost being, rest your mind on all the positive things you want to achieve in your children and life as a whole.

3. Harness every repetitive task

There are many boring routines. You can take advantage of these boring routines and use auto-suggestion. Many people love to use auto-suggestion when they are taking their baths, driving or cooking. This bathroom or shower style will be helpful if you are the kind that barely has time to sit and do something out of the schedule.

Choose what you want to dwell on for each shower or cooking session. If your kid is ill and you need him to recover, take that and perform positive thinking and affirmations on it. For the entire bathing session or a good portion of it say things like "my son is healed", 'you are back on your feet', 'I can see you run around like you used to'. Dwell on it and let your mind travel to heal your boy.

4. Engage your emotions

Emotions are potent when applied. We love our children and engaging that passion will help us achieve faster results. The rate at which your auto-suggestion works is directly proportional to the depth at which the situation touches you.

Having dysfunctional kids can be frustrating and seeing your child in a devastating state can be painful. The good thing is that pain is not for nothing. Engage that pain with auto-suggestion to get the result you have been seeking. You will be surprised at the speed of your answers.

5. Use it to influence every area of your life

Auto-suggestion does not only work for children. These techniques can affect every aspect of your life and make life easier and better. As a parent or guardian, you know there are times you unleash anger on your kids when they are not even wrong. This transfer of aggression makes it difficult to be a proper parent. However, auto-suggestion can help make life and parenting easy. Here is how:

If you have started using auto-suggestion, you will realize that it works as an antidote for every anger and frustration. When you deal with all your pains and anger with auto-suggestion, there will be nothing left to hurt your children.

So, to use this auto-suggestion to improve your life, take out some time to treat each goal. Sit in a quiet place and connect to your inner voice, open the door to your imagination and visualize how you have achieved your goal. Let the mental picture be clear and detailed, and try to include your five senses in this act. To round up every purpose, use a positive affirmation.

If you do this for about ten minutes each day, they will work for you.

CHAPTER 12 - USING MINDFULNESS TO RESPOND INSTEAD OF REACTING

S tress is now becoming very common, and it is one of the most common reasons we act instead if responding to our children. When the body encounters stress or danger, the brain sends a signal to the body alarm system called the amygdala, which in response causes our body to react without really considering our reactions. This impulsive reaction should be a shield to us, but since the scenarios with our children are not dangerous, we hurt them with our swift reaction.

Responding to children grooms love and healing; this means that reacting in cases we were supposed to respond can cause them emotional pain and trauma. Reacting badly to children can be the determining factor if you turn out to be the best parent in the world or memory, they try to forget.

Most times, reacting to children has so much to do with us as parents than the children. Here is what I mean: the way you were parented has a lot to do with how you will parent your children, so if you had reactive parents, you would be reactive except you take measures to change that. So, it does not really matter what your children did wrong, if you do not learn how to respond, you will end up destroying your relationship with your kid.

I met with a great mum, and this is what she had to say about her reactive behavior: "I find myself reacting and screaming at my girl whenever I get back from work, I just end up sending her to her room, and the joy between us just ends! I feel like this habit is pushing her away from me". According to this mum, she had a reactive mum who she felt never took her time to listen. This is same. Reacting to your children will create a gap in understanding.

Here is how you can switch from reacting to responding to your children:

1. Consider your childhood

Remember when mum never considered listening to the second time to anything you had to say? I do, and I felt she was really unreasonable. This feeling must have really made us hurt, and to some, it left scars.

Your childhood has a stronghold on how you parent your child. Take your time to reflect on it. What did you get from your parents, was it always a response or reaction? How did it make you feel? Do not forget your parents may have reacted with no bad intentions, so this will make you prone to reacting even when you do cherish your child.

Write down how your parents reacting made you feel like a child, and ponder on it to understand the effect of your reaction to your child.

2. Learn your triggers

Do not forget that stress plays a significant role in reacting to your kids. When your stress level is high, you will tend to react to some specific things. Take your mind back; when do you tend to shout and react most? Is it during dinner or shower time? Could it be their questioning after work?

To succeed at responding instead of reacting, you will need to learn what pulls out that beast and be conscious of it. If your triggers set off after work, then be very mindful when you are coming back home, ensure you find ways to calm yourself whenever it feels like you are about to lose it.

3. Learn possible ways to change the patterns of the past

The past cannot be changed, but we can change the way it influences the future. If you had responsive parents, learn from them. You can ask them how they had so much self-control and if you had reactive parents, find other responses that can substitute your reaction.

If your child gets you losing your mind, you can decide to walk away for some time until you gain control. Instead of shouting, you should try the next step.

4. **Practice self-control**

Being responsive has so much to do with the amount of control you have over yourself. This self-control will help you keep calm when everything in you wants to scream. Restraint will also help you realise that your kids are great, and they just need a little bit of patience from you to be more significant.

You must have some self-control strategies that help you get through your day to day activities; apply them whenever you start feeling the symptoms of anger.

5. Take deep breaths and count one to ten

The emotion behind reacting to a child is anger, and when you conquer anger, you have conquered all. When it feels like your anger is rising, take some deep breaths and count one to ten. You can draw three deep breaths before counting one to ten. If relying on one to ten does not relieve your anger, try counting it backwards; i.e. 10 − 1. The deep rush of oxygen and the time taken will help you relax while considering what to say to the child.

Finally

You will never understand how your children feel by watching them from a distance. To learn the heartbeat of your children, you will have to get close and commit yourself to be the best parent they could have ever had.

FINAL REMARK

Everyone knows that raising children is not the most straightforward job in the world; but as parents, we must be determined to get our children to the height we want them to reach. One of the ways of getting them to that height is through discipline.

We have discussed many discipline strategies, but you are the one who knows which suits your child better. If the suitable method for your child is not here but works, go on. All I can advise is that you watch out for when to stop or change the technique. What worked for a toddler will not work for a teenager.

Our kids are our treasures, and as God would have it; they will always be the most important one. Grooming them to become the best is the best gift we can offer them as parents, and when their lives turn out well, they will forever be grateful to us.

This job is no child's play, you back will ache, and you will forget what it feels like to have a good sleep, but at the end of the day, you will realize that your joy was attached to those things that seemed like they were extremely stressful.

May you reap the fruit of this labor. Amen.

Printed in Great Britain
by Amazon